Twenty to Make

Celtic Jewellery

Amanda W

Search Press

First published in Great Britain 2010

Search Press Limited
Wellwood, North Farm Road,
Tunbridge Wells, Kent TN2 3DR

Text copyright © Amanda Walker 2010

Photographs by Debbie Patterson at
Search Press Studios

Photographs and design copyright
© Search Press Ltd 2010

ISBN-13: 978-1-84448-456-0

Suppliers
If you have difficulty in obtaining any of the
materials and equipment mentioned in this book,
then please visit the Search Press website for
details of suppliers: www.searchpress.com

Printed in Malaysia

Dedication
For my Mum, Peggy Smith.

Contents

Introduction

Designing and making Celtic jewellery gives you the opportunity to explore a whole variety of jewellery-making techniques, from stringing beads to tying decorative knots, or casting solid silver pieces in precious metal clay.

Most of the pieces in this book need very little equipment and are very easy to make, but for those of you who need a challenge, there are projects that will take longer and require a little patience. Hopefully the easier projects will spur you on to create the more intricate pieces, which I hope you find very rewarding.

Once you have finished the projects in this book, why not try designing your own Celtic jewellery? I suggest you look through all of your craft-making kit – not just your jewellery pieces – and start looking at the items in it in a different way. A brad or an eyelet could be just the right colour to incorporate in your design, for example. Just remember to look outside the box when putting together a jewellery design.

Finally, I hope you enjoy the book and learn a few new techniques. I have included a range of projects, so I hope to offer you the opportunity to discover something that you have not yet tried. Go on, have a go, there is something in here for everyone!

Materials and template

There is a huge array of beautiful beads available for a variety of different uses, from metal divider beads to beautiful handmade glass beads.

Beads and all related products such as findings (all the pieces needed to connect and assemble the jewellery, such as head pins, eye pins and fastenings) are readily available in department stores and specialist craft shops. They are also easily bought online, making the whole world accessible to you without leaving your home.

Scrapbooking and cardmaking products – such as beautiful ribbons, stunning papers, felt flowers and buttons – mix well with jewellery components. The colours used in this type of product and the accompanying components are beautifully coordinated and well designed.

Most of the designs in this book incorporate cord, so look for beads with large enough threading holes to accommodate the cord or leather lacing and hunt out interesting cords and lacing which also are available in a huge range of finishes, colours and weights, giving your finished pieces an unique individual quality.

Template for the *Clover Earrings* and *Clover Necklace* projects

This template is reproduced at actual size. See pages 14 and 44 for the projects.

Knot diagrams

Knot diagram for the *Knotted Necklace* and *Knotted Bracelet* projects

See pages 12 and 40 for the projects.

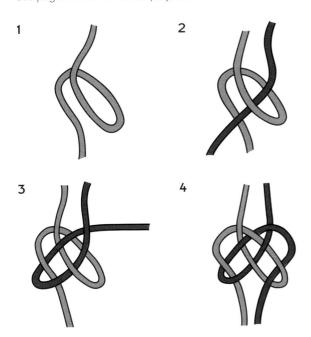

Knot diagram for the *Corded Bracelet* project

The white cord is a lazy cord. Keep it central throughout the knotting process. See page 16 for the project.

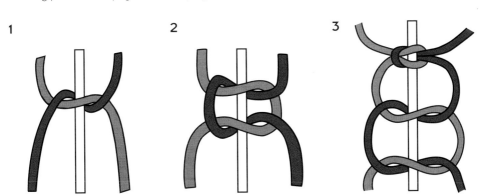

Emerald Earrings

Materials:

2 x earring hooks
4 x cord end caps
12cm (4¾in) of satin cord
4 x silver jump rings
2 x silver head pins
2 x silver metal beads

Tools:

Flat-nosed pliers
Round-nosed pliers
Wire cutters
Scissors

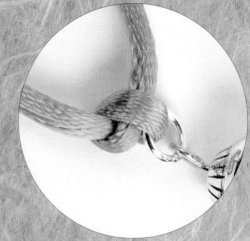

Instructions:

1 Thread a head pin with a silver metal bead. Using the flat-nosed pliers, bend the wire to a right angle and then cut, leaving 1cm (½in) of wire above the bead.

2 Using the round-nosed pliers, bend the wire into a loop. Just before the loop is fully closed, thread on a closed jump ring.

3 Cut the cord in half and then thread one piece through the jump ring and tie a simple overhand knot in the centre of the cord (see detail).

4 Attach cord end caps to each end of the cord and then attach the end caps to a jump ring. Whilst the jump ring is open attach the earring hook.

5 Repeat the process to complete the pair.

Morrow-wind

*These earrings are made in the same way,
using an alternative bead and a rich red
cord to evoke a Welsh feel.*

Trinity Bag Charm

Materials:
65cm (25½in) of brown fine
  glazed cotton cord
1 x large cord end cap
1 x silver divider metal bead
3 x silver head pins
1 x silver metal bead
1 x Chinese knot bead
1 x troll bead
4 x silver spin top beads
1 x silver jump ring
1 x silver carabiner

Tools:
Flat-nosed pliers
Round-nosed pliers
Wire cutters
Scissors
Jewellery glue

Instructions:

1 Thread a head pin with a silver spin top metal bead, the
Chinese knot bead and another spin top bead. Using the flat-
nosed pliers, bend the wire to a right angle and then cut, leaving
1cm (½in) of wire above the bead. Using the round-nosed pliers,
bend the wire into a loop.

2 Repeat this process with the troll bead.

3 Repeat this process with the metal bead, omitting the spin
top beads.

4 Divide and cut the cord into three equal pieces. Thread each
of the assembled beads on to one of the pieces of cord then
move each bead to the centre of its cord.

5 Double the cords; draw all the ends together and thread on
the metal divider bead. Push the metal bead down the cords to
sit above the beads.

6 Divide the cords into three and then make a 4cm (1¾in) plait
(see detail). Add glue to the top of the plait to secure it, trim the
cords to the same length and then attach a cord end cap.

7 Finally, attach the carabiner with a jump ring.

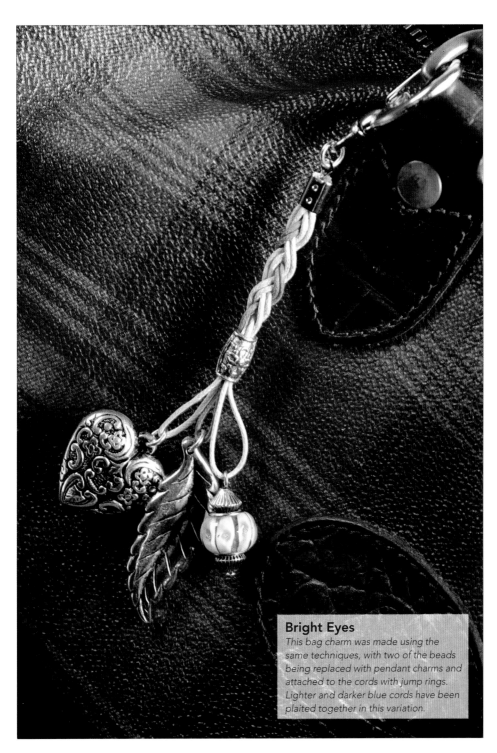

Bright Eyes

This bag charm was made using the same techniques, with two of the beads being replaced with pendant charms and attached to the cords with jump rings. Lighter and darker blue cords have been plaited together in this variation.

Knotted Necklace

Materials:

100cm (39¼in) black artificial suede lace

60cm (23½in) green artificial
   suede lace

1 x Chinese knot bead

10 x metal divider beads

2 x large silver cord end caps

2 x silver jump rings

1 x silver lobster hook fastening

Tools:

Flat-nosed pliers

Round-nosed pliers

Jewellery glue

Scissors

Instructions:

1 Cut the black lace in half, then thread the Chinese knot bead on to the centre of the laces. Thread a divider metal bead on each side of the Chinese bead.

2 Next follow the diagrams to make a Celtic knot (see page 7) on each side of the large bead close to the tubular metal beads.

3 Cut the green lace in half and use these to weave through the Celtic knot, starting at the top of the knot, following the pattern of the black knot (see detail).

4 Thread a divider bead on to the two black laces and push it up close to the knot. Divide the laces into two pairs of one black and one green each. Thread a divider bead on to each pair. Glue the pairs of green and black laces together 2cm (¾in) above the first set of divider beads and then cut the green laces. Slide the two divider beads over the glued areas.

5 Thread another divider bead on to the two black laces and then repeat the process on the opposite side of the necklace.

6 Trim the lace ends to the same length; attach cord end caps and then two jump rings and a lobster fastening.

Thistlewick

The same knotwork has been worked to make this necklace, but finer cord has been used, which creates a more delicate effect. In addition, the final divider bead (see step 5 opposite) has been left off the cord, allowing the cord to play lightly around the neck.

13

Clover Earrings

Materials:

2 x silver earring hooks

Double-sided scrapbooking paper

2 x silver jump rings

2 x silver head pins

2 x silver metal beads

Tools:

Flat-nosed pliers

Round-nosed pliers

Small hole punch

Wire cutters

Scissors

Jewellery glue

Nail varnish

Instructions:

1 From the template provided (see page 6) cut out four clover shapes from the scrapbooking paper.

2 Place a narrow line of glue down the centre of one and stick another to it, making sure matching designs are on the facing sides (see detail).

3 Use the hole punch to make small holes at the base of the stalk and at the top of the clover.

4 Thread a head pin with a silver metal bead. Using the flat-nosed pliers, bend the wire to a right angle and then cut, leaving 1cm (½in) of wire above the bead.

5 Using the round-nosed pliers, bend the wire into a loop. Just before the loop is fully closed thread it through the hole in the stalk of the clover.

6 Use a jump ring to attach an earring hook to the top of the clover. Dot the joins in the jump rings with clear nail varnish to prevent the clovers being lost and then bend the clover leaves out to create a three-dimensional effect.

7 Repeat the process to complete the pair.

Amongst the Grass

These earrings use glass droplet beads instead of metal beads for a simple and cheery alternative.

15

Corded Bracelet

Materials:

150cm (60in) of 3mm
   (⅛in) cotton
   braided cord
Large metal bead

Tools:

Heavyweight pins
   and cushion
Scissors
Jewellery glue

Instructions:

1 Cut a 35cm (13¾in) length from the cord and pin the
end to a cushion; this cord runs through the centre of
the knotting.

2 Double the remainder of the cord and pin the centre point
below the single piece of cord, creating a loop.

3 Follow the diagrams on page 7 to create approximately 7cm
(2¾in) of flat knots (essentially a series of reef knots) tied around
the central cord.

4 Thread the bead on to the central cord and continue knotting
on the other side of the bead. The length of the knotting will
depend on the size of your wrist.

5 Bring the three cords together and tie a single knot. Cut the
cords near to the knot, then place glue on the cord ends and
tuck them under the last flat knot (see detail). This side becomes
the back of the bracelet. Cut and glue the single central cord at
the beginning of the bracelet in the same way.

Ladystone
Using a round braided bead to replace the metal bead gives a more feminine effect, but one that is equally striking.

Spiral Earrings

Materials:

50cm (19¾in) of silk-covered wire

2 x spin top metal beads

2 x earring hooks

Tools:

Flat-nosed pliers

Wire cutters

Wire mandrel

Instructions:

1 Starting at a wider point of the wire mandrel, wind the wire around to the narrow end. Take the spiralled wire off the mandrel and cut it, leaving a 1.5cm (¾in) tail.

2 Thread on the small spin top bead and then using the flat-nosed pliers bend the wire end up into the end of the spiral.

3 At the top of the spiral, bend the top round at a right angle, thread an earring hook on to the end of the wire and then tuck the end down inside the spiral (see detail).

4 Repeat the process to complete the pair.

Eternal Spiral

These earrings have been made in a different coloured wire, slightly shorter in length and have small metal crosses added to replace the spin top beads.

19

Heart Necklace

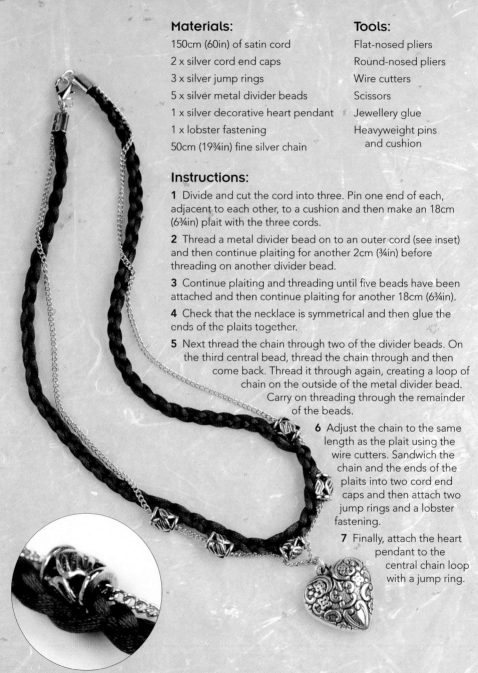

Materials:

150cm (60in) of satin cord
2 x silver cord end caps
3 x silver jump rings
5 x silver metal divider beads
1 x silver decorative heart pendant
1 x lobster fastening
50cm (19¾in) fine silver chain

Tools:

Flat-nosed pliers
Round-nosed pliers
Wire cutters
Scissors
Jewellery glue
Heavyweight pins
  and cushion

Instructions:

1 Divide and cut the cord into three. Pin one end of each, adjacent to each other, to a cushion and then make an 18cm (6¾in) plait with the three cords.

2 Thread a metal divider bead on to an outer cord (see inset) and then continue plaiting for another 2cm (¾in) before threading on another divider bead.

3 Continue plaiting and threading until five beads have been attached and then continue plaiting for another 18cm (6¾in).

4 Check that the necklace is symmetrical and then glue the ends of the plaits together.

5 Next thread the chain through two of the divider beads. On the third central bead, thread the chain through and then come back. Thread it through again, creating a loop of chain on the outside of the metal divider bead. Carry on threading through the remainder of the beads.

6 Adjust the chain to the same length as the plait using the wire cutters. Sandwich the chain and the ends of the plaits into two cord end caps and then attach two jump rings and a lobster fastening.

7 Finally, attach the heart pendant to the central chain loop with a jump ring.

Courage
Using a royal blue cord and a leaf pendant creates a Scottish feel to the necklace.

Votive Bracelet

Materials:

30cm (12in) of beading elastic

15 x 8mm metal round beads

1 x silver jump ring

1 x silver decorative metal rectangular bead

1 x metal cross pendant

Tools:

Flat-nosed pliers

Round-nosed pliers

Scissors

Jewellery glue

Instructions:

1 Thread the 30cm (12in) length of beading elastic with fifteen round metal beads, and then a silver rectangular bead.

2 Tie the two ends of the elastic together with a reef knot, pulling the beads up tightly as you tie. Dot the knot with glue and leave to dry.

3 When the glue is dry, trim the ends of the elastic and then pull the knot inside the silver rectangular metal bead.

4 Attach the metal cross to the side of the rectangular bead with a jump ring.

Blackwood

For a stronger, bolder look, replace the round metal beads with wooden rectangular beads.

Button Necklace

Materials:

50cm (19¾in) of decorative ribbon
50cm (19¾in) of lilac suede lace
3 x green mother-of-pearl buttons
4 x silver metal divider beads
2 x silver cord end caps
2 x silver jump rings
1 x silver lobster fastening

Tools:

Flat-nosed pliers
Round-nosed pliers
Needle and matching thread
Jewellery glue
Scissors
Iron

Instructions:

1 Place the tip of the iron on one side of the ribbon and then pull the ribbon tightly into a curve as you iron along the ribbon. Aim to develop a curve in it.

2 Thread four metal divider beads on to the lilac lace, spacing them 4cm (1½in) apart, starting from the centre of the lace.

3 Place the lace on top of the ribbon and then stitch a button, through the lace and into the ribbon, in between each of the divider beads.

4 Glue the lace to the ribbon in a few places to secure.

5 Cut the ends to equal lengths. Sandwich the lace and the ends of the ribbon into two cord end caps (see detail) and then attach two jump rings and a lobster fastening.

Bold as Buttons

This alternative to the more delicate necklace opposite is made with bold decorative silver buttons, a narrow organza ribbon, fine braid and tiny silver beads.

Leaf Bracelet

Materials:
17 x 8mm silver jump rings
5 x silver eye pins
5 x 8mm round silver metal beads
1 x silver leaf pendant
1 x silver lobster fastening
1 x silver heart extension chain

Tools:
Flat-nosed pliers
Round-nosed pliers
Wire cutters
Jewellery glue

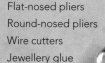

Instructions:

1 Make a jump ring chain by linking eight jump rings together.

2 Before closing the last jump ring, thread on an eye pin then thread this pin with a round metal bead. Using the flat-nosed pliers, bend the wire to a right angle and then cut, leaving 1cm (½in) of wire above the bead.

3 Using the round-nosed pliers, bend the wire into a loop. Just before the loop is fully closed thread on another eye pin and repeat the process four more times.

4 After the fifth bead has been joined attach another length of jump ring chain (made in the same way as in step 1, but with nine jump rings), then attach the leaf pendant to the first jump ring.

5 Finally, attach a lobster fastening to one end of the chain and an extension chain to the other.

Pearl Years

Small 4mm jump rings have been used to create the chain, while mother-of-pearl droplet beads replace the round metal beads, giving colour and a different feel to the bracelet.

27

Pendant Necklace

Materials:

16cm (6¼in) of lilac suede lace
1 x silver head pin
1 x silver spin top bead
2 x silver divider silver metal beads
1 x large silver decorative bead
1 x silver 8mm round bead
1 x silver cord end cap

Tools:

Flat-nosed pliers
Round-nosed pliers
Wire cutters
Jewellery glue

Instructions:

1 Attach a cord end cap to one end of the lilac lace.

2 Thread a head pin with a silver spin top metal bead, a large decorative bead and the round 8mm metal bead. Using the flat-nosed pliers, bend the wire to a right angle and then cut, leaving 1cm (½in) of wire above the bead. Using the round-nosed pliers, bend the wire into a loop. Before the loop is fully closed attach to the end cap.

3 Thread on a metal divider bead. This bead is used to cover the end cap (see detail).

4 Thread another divider metal bead on to the other end of the lace. Bend the end of the lace into a loop; dot the end with glue and then push the end into the divider bead. This loop is used to fasten the necklace – simply slip it over the large bead.

Light Hearted

A green cord with a heart pendant attached makes for a beautiful Irish-themed keepsake. It was made with fewer beads and a jump ring, and was completed using the same methods.

Band of Lovers

Materials:

40cm (15¾in) of
   decorative ribbon

2 x silver ribbon end caps

1 x silver decorative
   heart pendant

2 x silver metal divider beads

2 x silver jump rings

1 x silver lobster fastening

12cm (4¾in) of satin cord

Tools:

Flat-nosed pliers

Round-nosed pliers

Scissors

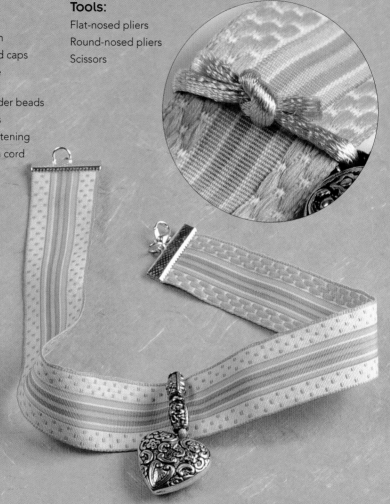

Instructions:

1 Cut the ribbon to sit comfortably around your neck and then attach the ribbon end caps.

2 Thread the heart pendant and the two metal divider beads on to the piece of satin cord.

3 Wrap the cord ends around the centre of the ribbon and tie in a reef knot on the back of the ribbon (see detail).

4 Attach a jump ring to each of the ribbon end caps and a lobster fastening to one of the jump rings.

Pastel Piece

For an alternative design, make up a choker on a narrower piece of ribbon and add a small metal cross pendant with a single bead above it.

Felt Bead Bracelet

Materials:

4 x felt beads

8 x 8mm round metal beads

3 x silver drum eye
  divider beads

3 x jump rings

2 x silver calottes

1 x silver decorative ring
  and bar clasp

3 x small silver metal charms

Beading thread

Tools:

Round-nosed pliers

Scissors

Beading needle

Jewellery glue

Instructions:

1 Attach each of the three charms to a drum eye bead with a jump ring (see detail).

2 Thread a beading needle with approximately 100cm (39¼in) of thread. Place the two ends together to make the thread doubled and then tie a couple of knots.

3 Thread on a calotte, dot the knot with glue and then close the calotte around the knot. Trim away any excess thread.

4 Thread on a round metal bead, a felt bead, another metal bead and then a drum eye bead.

Repeat this process twice and then thread on a round metal bead, the last felt bead and the remaining round metal bead.

5 Thread on a calotte, cut the thread near to the needle and remove. Pull the beads up tightly as you tie the threads in a knot inside the calotte. Make another couple of knots, dot with glue, close the calotte and trim away the excess thread.

6 Finally attach the ring and bar clasps to the calottes.

Silver Earth

Here, the felt beads have been replaced with beautiful handmade glass beads and two different charms.

Cross Necklace

Materials:
9gm (¼oz) of PMC 3 silver clay

100cm (39¼in) of black
   suede lace

1 x silver jump ring

Celtic cross rubber stamp

Tools:
Playing cards

Small rolling pin

Butane pencil blow torch

Touch mat and block

Olive oil

Craft knife

Emery board

Wire brush

Burnishing tool

Polishing cloth

Instructions:

1 Rub both sides of a playing card with a little olive oil and place it on your surface.

2 Make two piles of three playing cards. Place the piles on to the surface, one on either side of the oiled playing card.

3 Place the clay on to the oiled card and then roll the clay out between the playing cards. Lift the clay and roll again. The cards will determine the thickness of the clay (the two piles of playing cards raise the rolling pin, so an even thickness of clay is created).

4 Place the rubber stamp over the clay and press down.

5 Cut around the shape with a craft knife, make a small hole at the top of the cross and leave until bone dry. When the clay is totally dry carefully sand the edges with the emery board.

6 Place the dried cross on to the tile and fire with the butane torch until the clay glows red for ten seconds. Leave to cool.

7 Use a wire brush to remove the white layer from the clay and reveal the silver below.

8 Use the burnishing tool and the polishing cloth to polish the surface of the cross and make it sparkle.

9 Attach a jump ring through the hole in the cross (see detail opposite), then hang it from a piece of black knotted lace.

Interlocking

The alternatives to a cross are endless. Use different rubber stamps to make different patterns and shapes.

Braided Bracelet

Materials:

100cm (39¼in) of black satin cord

3 x green troll beads

2 x silver cord end caps

2 x silver jump rings

1 x silver decorative ring and bar clasp

Tools:

Flat-nosed pliers

Round-nosed pliers

Heavyweight pins and cushion

Jewellery glue

Scissors

Instructions:

1 Divide and cut the cord into three. Pin the ends to a cushion and then make a 20cm (7¾in) plait with the three cords (see detail).

2 Glue the ends of the plait and leave to dry.

3 Trim away the excess cord and attach an end cap to one end.

4 Thread on the three troll beads and attach the remaining end cap.

5 Attach the ring and bar clasp with jump rings.

Circle of Life

This plaited bracelet can be embellished with a variety of different types of bead. Vibrant emerald green and silver beads are perfect together.

Bluebell Brooch

Materials:

2 x large felt flowers in aqua and cream
1 x large organza flower
1 x smaller lilac felt flower
1 x aqua paper flower
1 x small pink button
1 x silver metal cross
1 x silver brooch back pin

Tools:

Needle and matching thread

Instructions:

1 Layer the flowers up in size order, from the largest felt flower to the small paper flower.

2 Thread the needle, double the thread and tie a knot in the ends of the doubled thread. Pass the needle through from the back of the largest flower to the centre of the paper flower.

3 Thread on the metal cross and then the pink button. Pass the needle back through the button and through to the back of the largest felt flower.

4 Knot the thread off securely and then stitch the brooch pin to the back of the flower (see detail).

Pennyflower

These brooches are made from scrapbooking products. I have found these a fantastic source of inspiration for jewellery-making.

Knotted Bracelet

Materials:

60cm (23½in) of green satin cord
60cm (23½in) of blue satin cord
2 x silver cord end caps
2 x silver jump rings
1 x silver decorative ring and bar clasp

Tools:

Flat-nosed pliers
Round-nosed pliers
Scissors
Large pin and cushion
Jewellery glue

Instructions:

1 Cut the two pieces of cord in half and pin them in two sets of blue and green and green and blue on to a cushion. Follow the diagram to make a Celtic knot (see page 7) in the centre of the cords.

2 Cut and glue the cord ends to equal lengths to fit comfortably around your wrist.

3 Attach a cord end cap to each end, then attach the ring and bar clasp to the end caps using jump rings.

Knot of Dragons

This is a good opportunity to experiment with colour. Use cords with contrasting colours or be subtle and tone the colours.

Flower Necklace

Materials:

60cm (23½in) of red satin cord
2 x lilac small felt flowers
1 x green small felt flower
1 x pink covered button brads
2 x green covered button brads
4 x silver flower pendants
2 x silver cord end caps
1 x silver lobster fastening
2 x silver jump rings

Tools:

Flat-nosed pliers
Round-nosed pliers
Scissors

Instructions:

1 Place the centre of the satin cord in between the prongs of the covered button brad. Push the prongs through the centre of the green felt flower; you may need to make a small cut in the centre of the flower and then open out the prongs.

2 Thread two flower pendants, one either side of the flower. Tie knots in the cord to secure the pendants 2cm (¾in) away from the flower (see detail).

3 Next attach two more flowers and buttons, again 2cm (¾in) away from the flower pendants and then another two flower pendants again knotted to secure them in place.

4 Trim the cords to make the necklace symmetrical, attach end caps to the cord ends and then finally attach two jump rings with the lobster fastening attached to one of them.

Flower of Youth

This necklace features just one larger flower with the four flower pendants knotted on to the cord.

Clover Necklace

Materials:

Double-sided scrapbooking paper

10 x silver jump rings

3 x silver ball-ended head pins

3 x freshwater pearls

60cm (23½in) of 3mm lilac
satin ribbon

40cm (15¾in) of silver chain

1 x silver lobster fastening

Tools:

Flat-nosed pliers

Round-nosed pliers

Wire cutters

Scissors

Jewellery glue

Small hole punch

Clear nail varnish

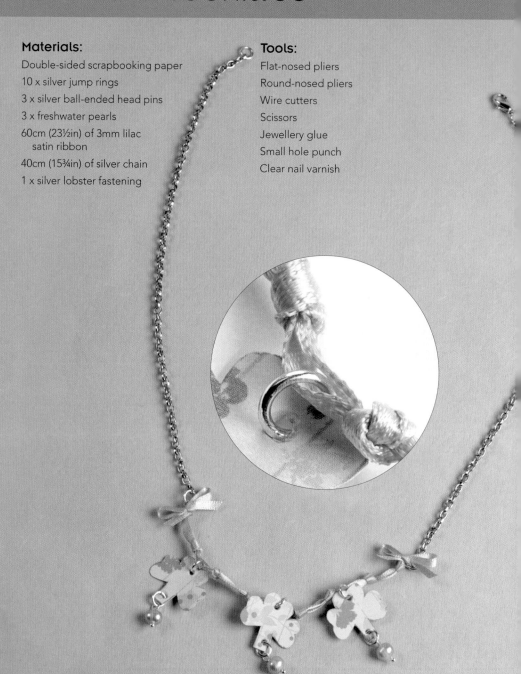

Instructions:

1 From the template provided (see page 6) cut out three clover shapes from the scrapbooking paper.

2 Make a hole at the base of the stalk and another at the top of the clover using the small hole punch. Attach a jump ring to the hole in the stalk.

3 Thread a head pin with a freshwater pearl. Using the flat-nosed pliers, bend the wire to a right angle and then cut, leaving 1cm (½in) of wire above the bead.

4 Using the round-nosed pliers, bend the wire into a loop. Just before the loop is fully closed thread it through the jump ring in the stalk of the clover.

5 Repeat the process to make up two more clovers and attach a jump ring to each of the holes in the top of the leaves. Dot all the joins

in the jump rings with clear nail varnish to prevent the clovers being lost.

6 Cut the ribbon in half and thread a clover on to the centre of one piece of ribbon. Take the other piece, lay it over the first and then tie a knot either side of the clover in both of them.

7 Leave a 1cm (½in) space between the knots and tie another and attach the remaining two assembled clovers in the same way. Leave another 1cm (½in) gap and then tie a knot.

8 Cut the chain in half and attach a jump ring to each of the ends. Thread the ribbon ends through the jump rings and tie in bows. Trim the tails of the bows and then dot the centre of the bows with glue.

9 Finally attach the clasp of the lobster fastening to one of the jump rings at the other end of the chain.

Chimes of Spring

Scrapbooking papers come in a fantastic range of designs and this necklace's components have been matched to the subtle tones of the paper.

Lucky Charm

Materials:

1 x silver decorative round metal bead
1 x oblong decorative metal bead
1 x square handmade glass bead
5 x 3mm glass faceted beads
3 x silver head pins
1 x 8mm silver jump ring
12cm (4¾in) of silver chain
1 x silver carabiner

Tools:

Flat-nosed pliers
Round-nosed pliers
Wire cutters

Instructions:

1 Cut the chain into three pieces, making them slightly different lengths.

2 Thread the three head pins with the three large beads; place a small glass faceted bead at the base and top of the large glass and metal oblong beads and just one above the round metal bead.

3 Using the flat-nosed pliers, bend the wires to right angles and then cut, leaving 1cm (½in) of wire above the beads.

4 Using the round-nosed pliers, bend the wires into a loop. Just before the loops are fully closed, thread through the links at the ends of the three pieces of chain.

5 Open the jump ring and thread on the tops of the chain ends and before closing the jump ring thread on the carabiner.

Good Luck Charm
The alternative has a more rustic feel incorporating china and small metal spin top beads.

Acknowledgements

Special thanks to Julie Pirie and my sister Jody Dimes for giving me their time and help to complete this book. Edd Ralph, my editor, for making the process of producing this book simple for me. Thanks also to the photographer Debbie Patterson for her beautiful pictures and all at Search Press for giving me this opportunity.